Howie Abrams & Michael "Kaves" McLeer

Foreword by Darryl "DMC" McDaniels

PERMUTED
PRESS

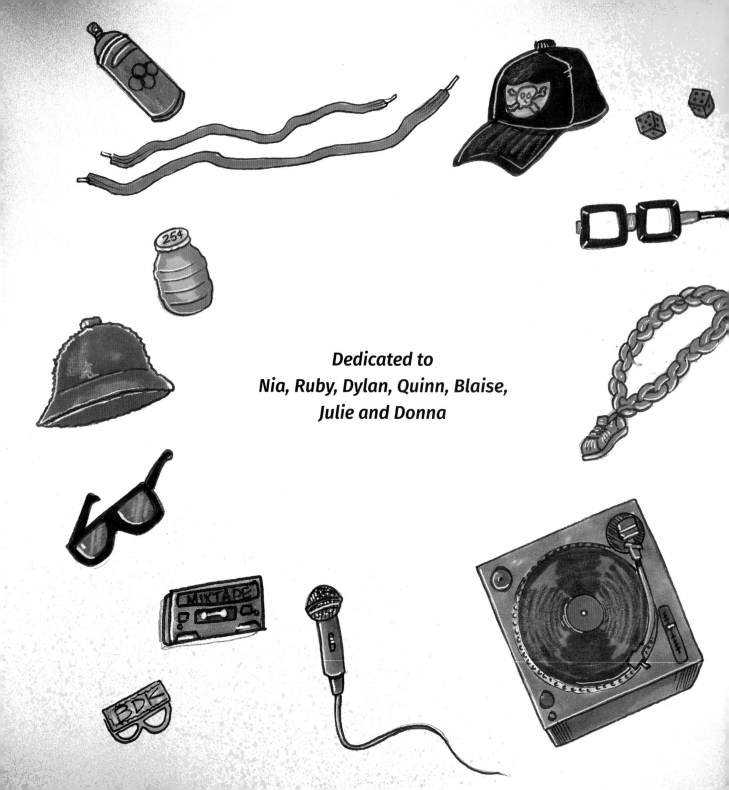

Dedicated to
Nia, Ruby, Dylan, Quinn, Blaise,
Julie and Donna

FOREWORD

Books are a great way to bring adults and children together, from helping young ones with schoolwork to reading kids bedtime stories. Hip-hop is also a wonderful way to teach. Many outstanding hip-hop storytellers have used their lyrics and flow to inspire and educate.

Hip-Hop Alphabet combines the wit and words of hip-hop with the artistic mastery of graffiti (our art) to provide a creative, educational experience for young and old alike. It's solid proof that hip-hop, as well as all of the arts, are powerful tools for learning—and educating our children!

—Darryl "DMC" McDaniels

A is for **A Tribe Called Quest,** Q-Tip, Phife Dawg and Ali. Their laid-back rhymes over jazzy beats showed how chill hip-hop could be.

B is for Beastie Boys,
who gave us *Licensed to Ill*.
They fought for their right to party
and had the skills to pay the bills.

is for Cypress Hill,
Sen Dog, Muggs and B-Real.
They're insane in the membrane
with a West Coast Latino feel.

D is for DJs,
the architects of the sound.
They mix, fade and scratch
as the records spin around.

is for Fab 5 Freddy,
who mixed rap music with art.
He brought the uptown sound downtown,
helping hip-hop get its start.

G is for Graffiti,
made with markers and paint you spray.
You can see the tags on buildings,
billboards or the subway.

H is for House of Pain,
who love to jump around.
Their shamrocks and shenanigans
gave rap an Irish sound.

I is for Ice Cube,
who was in a group with Dr. Dre.
N.W.A came "Straight Outta Compton,"
putting the spotlight on L.A.

is for **Jay Z**,
who can rhyme fast or slow
with deep, insightful lyrics
and effortless Brooklyn flow.

is for **KRS One**,
a philosopher and a preacher.
He drops knowledge with his rhymes
and is hip-hop's greatest teacher.

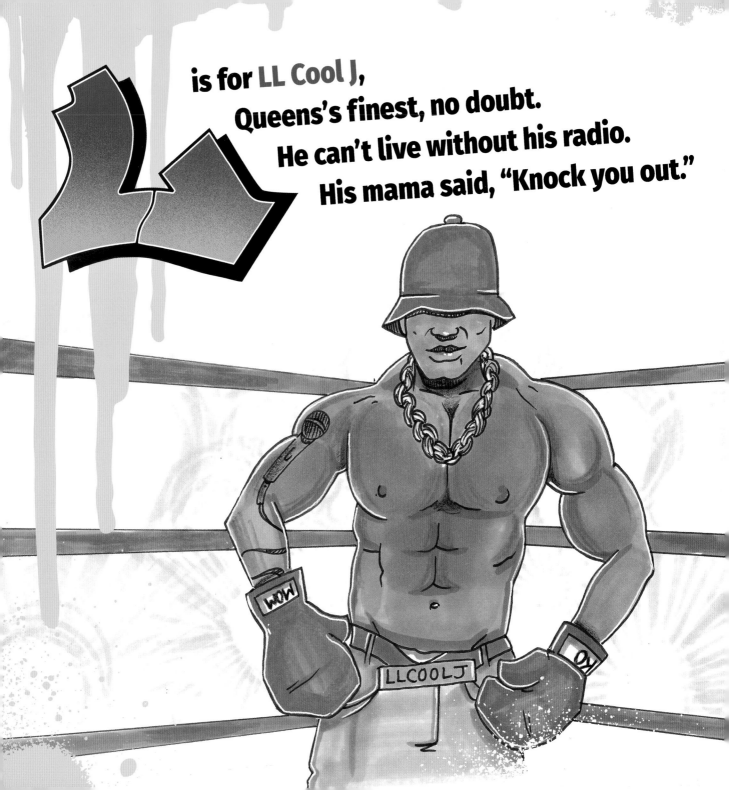

M is for Microphone, which makes a voice loud. It carries words from the stage out to everyone in the crowd.

is for The Notorious B.I.G.,
Biggie Smalls is his other name—
one of hip-hop's great lyricists
and the smoothest emcee in the game.

P is for Public Enemy,
who fight the power on every track.
Chuck D and Flavor Flav are still going strong.
A nation of millions can't hold them back.

Q is for Queen Latifah.
Onto the scene she burst
with the first female anthem,
singing "Ladies first, ladies first."

R is for **RUN DMC**.
They made rap a household name.
From 'round the way in Hollis, Queens,
to the Rock N Roll Hall of Fame.

RUN DMC

S is for **Snoop Dogg**,
whose rhymes always sizzle.
He invented his own rap language.
He's the D-O-double-Gizzle!

is for Tupac Shakur,
a rapper, actor and poet.
His lyrics presented a new point of view
and shaped hip-hop as we know it.

U is for the Underground,
from which this culture rose.
Its influence affected everything,
from music to sneakers to clothes.

V is for Vinyl,
which DJs carry in crates—
albums and 12-inch singles
that feature all the greats.

X is for Xzibit,
an emcee and television host.
He loves his wacky cars
and drives them on the West Coast.

Y is for Yo! MTV Raps,
the most popular hip-hop show on TV.
They played videos by rappers.
Now fans could listen and see.

Z is for Zigga Zigga.
This is what DJs found:
Scratching records back and forth
makes a beautiful sound.

ACKNOWLEDGEMENTS

Howie and Kaves would like to thank:
Jacob Hoye, Michael Croland, Lesser Gods,
Donna McLeer, DMC, Erik Blam, Joseph Gargano, Bella Kozyreva

A portion of the proceeds from *Hip-Hop Alphabet* will be donated to the Jam Master Jay Foundation for Music. The foundation operates under the simple premise that regardless of socio-economic status, every child deserves equal access to the arts. The foundation supports the idea that social Justice, Arts and Music (J.A.M.) education should be in every school, in every region of the country, giving children the opportunity to expand their worldview through artistic expression.

www.JamMasterJay.org

ABOUT THE AUTHORS

Howie used to work in the music biz
at record labels and such.
Now he is an author,
who loves his family very much.

Kaves is a legendary graffiti artist
and a renaissance man.
He's toured all around the world
with his Lordz of Brooklyn band.

A PERMUTED PRESS BOOK
ISBN: 978-1-68261-8-660

Published by arrangement with Overamstel Publishers, Inc.

Design by Donna McLeer

PERMUTED PRESS

Permuted Press, LLC
New York • Nashville
permutedpress.com

Published in the United States of America
Printed in China